Root Rot

Root Rot
Copyright © 2023 Rhienna Renée Guedry
All rights reserved. First Edition.

Cooper Dillon Books
San Diego, California
CooperDillon.com

Cover Design & Interior by Adam Deutsch

ISBN: 978-1-943899-18-0

No part of this book may be reproduced without the publisher's written permission, except for brief quotations in reviews.

Root Rot

Rhienna Renée Guedry

Cooper Dillon

Table of Contents

MT. TABOR	1
CUT OFF, LA	2
THE SWAMP IS A THIRD-GENDER THING	3
THE NAME OF STREETS	5
SOME BONES ARE BLESSINGS	6
MILDEW	8
MERMAIDS	9
THE TRAIL WE TOOK INSTEAD OF THE OTHER ONE	10
UNTITLED GARDEN POEM	11
SMOKE WATER	12
ENTANGLEMENT	14
ART THERAPY	15
IT GETS YOU THROUGH	16
DISASTER PLANNING	17
AUGUST	18
THE YEAR I BROKE UP WITH THE MOON	20
FKA PLAQUEMINES	22
SOAK	24
COMPARTMENTS	25
TWO CAPTAINS	26
THIS CORROSION BEATS ON	28
I'M BACK AT URGENT CARE IN OVERALLS AGAIN	29
MICROCHIMERISM	30
FIRST THE GRASSHOPPER	31
WHAT HAPPENS TO THE BOXELDERS AFTER NOVEMBER	33
DEPARTURES	35
ACKNOWLEDGMENTS	37

MT. TABOR

You were a combustible thing. This overcast morning I ascend the site of a volcanic vent, where the neighborhood crows roost atop cinder cones. The reservoirs cup blue-green waters in a century-old expanse of stone and metal. Here where once was smolder and lava sits an urban park, crowned with a statue of a suited man, his finger an arrow aimed at the Willamette River. But enough about the park. I came here in pursuit of fire. Induction to extinction—
                        that described you, too. A rootless cavern burned through, persistent green proof of what flourishes after. You were thrilled by stories of pyroclastic flows, all spatter and tuff stuff. You lived for the heat, the ejecta; I am trying to, in your name.

CUT OFF, LA

the swamplands sound like a song & sound like police & sound like fish flopping on the line & sound like a bug zapper that texture of grass, mud, critters if the gators don't spot ya first, sure don't stick around to find out how long it takes them to what is that country song? "Ocean Front Property In Arizona?" the whole mess has nothin' on your #1 goal each night: finish the damn thing, find your way, be back home in time for supper. fold up, pack it in, nothing extra left behind: no faded candy bar wrapper stuck to a baseboard after a flood (take your best guess where the shortcut is in Cut Off) stay in love with the high grass & those fuchsia sunsets, the clay you call mud & the mudbugs you call crawfish you sent me a postcard after you left that read: *give Louisiana my greetings, tidings & regrets*

THE SWAMP IS A THIRD-GENDER THING

Point to where the firm edge of the river becomes marsh, where
a water route becomes one formerly known as:
land; river   sometimes the swamp is neither: a place
you might step onto but sometimes step right through,
sink right in, get those hairy knees wet loving this
other-category thing swamplands

are both,
and neither, inhabited by the living,

steered through
and landed on, all parted grasses, cypress domes
homes for under-water and above-water things

    be on your damn way
lest you start asking too many questions

their perfect position between both, as both
and neither, in exemplary excellence
when you know this, you know how to occupy
that space yourself
land and sea, green and brown, dry
but always drinking mostly wet,
say it,   thirsty
like swamps, storms will come and go
everything this humid defies static categories: weather,
    permaculture,
        land as uncertain as floodwaters inside a house where
water ain't supposed to be, a wild solstice thing
you know better than to sink your ankles in
when you've had too many whiskeys
the swamp is a shapeshifter from sci-fi:

they are the shoreline not the tide,
they are putting roots down,
they are licking oyster beds
because it's that season
                      kneel down on what is land
today but tomorrow may be water

THE NAME OF STREETS

Behind the Piggly Wiggly—moss in each live oak,
and a dewy gulch so fern-filled that for years
I thought it was a bonafide fairy glade
Later, I learned the steady trickle
was man-made: another canal to divert
the river, improve drainage and prevent flooding
to our suburb of the capitol, streets so named
for governance, so I skinned my knees
on Debit Drive, hopped chain-link fences
on Treasurer, looked for crawfish
in the ditches on Council

Raised in the same house for twelve
years and two floods, we spent year after year
chasing hot air balloons, outrunning hurricanes
when a final surrender came, *enough!*
We moved on, and then on again
five times in five years to another swamp,
another state—though never home to me,
just another wet place—another damp suburb
where I learned to spell *rhododendron*
and *chrysanthemum* not because I knew
their blooms, but because we moved
onto streets named after them, streets
where flowers used to grow

SOME BONES ARE BLESSINGS

I presumed something the size of a strawberry
would feel more like one in the crook of my hand, not
the orbit of little bones, a formerly-fast thing
now still, tongue a sword, all puff, pomp
of downy-green throat and competition.
Even at this size: machismo to duel,
to the death or to the pain. I learn the males
die this way just as often as they crash into glass.
I'd be lying if I told you I expected this.
What omen is he, for
us? To our delight, a good one. Prosperity, luck,
seven years in this house and still more with you;
a corpse to render our vows authentic.

    I.   Decaying methods: bury or
leave it be. I read online—
the suggestion: slide the hummingbird
into a stocking and bury him, to be
retrieved later like a gemstone. But
my aim has never unearthed
bulbs with a surgeon's precision.

    II.   Preservation: submerge or freeze. I think of
frozen berries; the friend who froze
their euthanized cat, though now I forget
why; the pretty snake takes her frozen
rats reheated, a pantomime of prey.

III. Instead: before spoils, spring
blooms around him, a crown in
lavender and cherry blossom, skylight
grey flash to pulse the hues of
green, tiny king, rich as peacocks.

IV. I bury the hummingbird under the lip
of our astroturf, near the jasmine. In spring the
ants march along. Weeks later, less than the bones of
an anchovy: just a stain.

MILDEW

We cut the bedroom walls at the four-foot seam
which gave us an education:
what size sheets of drywall come in,　　how high
flood waters get

that chalk-like powder is beneath
robin's egg blue paint

Understanding at twelve what rots,
what sags, what fades,
　　　　　　　what stinks, what you can get away with
not replacing
good thing no one in this family was a reader;
　　　　　　I'd have books
　　　　　　　　floating out the back door, me.

Some neighbors passed, saw us hauling
rotten carpet, a scene of spoiled
eggs and sewer and shouted
"Y'all back?"
　　　　　　Like,　　　*What's it look like?*
You can't forget the smell
that comes after　　it's how I learned mildew isn't a color
it's a texture, the raised level on a styrofoam cup
　　　condensation　　white pepper　　it changes
　　　with your fingerprints,
it reminds us that there is water under us all

MERMAIDS

Glacial homesteading,
that is until the floods came
and went and tossed
the four of us in motion
—you were as wet-wristed
 as Cher seeking new footing
on a map—an urgent sprint
to a state with no seasons

The ravine slipped underfoot
our homeland root-rotted, so we left
it behind, like a couch on the curb

Tiny brunette kingdom
of husband and daughters
whose pink plastic legs
you thundered
like we were the ones
running away, was that what
you most feared and perhaps,
most expected?

My youth's most Unreliable
Narrator—it was you
who did the leaving,
gave up on tracking river levels
against each of your hot flashes

When a mother stops wanting
to be one: a broom to a wasp's nest

Go faster. Go alone.
What choice did you give us

THE TRAIL WE TOOK INSTEAD OF THE OTHER ONE

Olive, cold   as soon as summer
      goes—here the rain   doesn't
all at once   like we're used to
instead, it leaks   a feast of drips
crocus mission   dewy, boots
at the back door gleam with warning:
     it really might rain every day that you're here

Our southern bones   glacial
       I'm acclimating, I say
I'm   the permanence
of ferns, my sips thick with
savory dampness   that glooms, this
delicious gesture
of bringing the boughs   in

I took you walking   forest deep
fate marching towards the
baby eagle we   found on the muddy trail
shock of   Shar Pei newness where feathers
would sprout   our instinct was to
put her back, as though   she had only
fallen from a shelf, passed
the five-second rule,
     bounced softly, and lived

UNTITLED GARDEN POEM
(Index: F.S. Pansy, Euphorbia)

Facing east, sunlight lingers out back as often as we do
to receive it, warming scalp and crown to tingle, squint
glint while the crows clean their beaks on our arbor,
having finished the scraps we feed them

We aspire for a garden that matches postcard
visions: poppies wild, shrubs fruitful, and still
we can't believe spring bulbs yield what they do, all
those days of grey and grey and grey and
sometimes soapy jade, from whence we barely
crawl out from underneath every April—that
was when the Frizzle Sizzle Pansies
I bought for you all died before May Day,
perhaps apt for a bloom with a name like that

The best plants are weeds, anyway
I transplant the Euphorbia—despite
your objections—because what I love is
its instinct: it doesn't need us
it doesn't need our attention
to survive

SMOKE WATER

Through plumes and evacuation
zones: the wildfires gave us
something else to look out for, large
and unmistakable
so we shifted our worry from
    danger to   danger
like weight, a baker's measure of volume,
as sure as eggs is eggs, a   fire is   fire,
so we prayed for rain, we studied the inversion
as it reversed   a mountain's tip
to thread its dark weather towards a valley; a heft that
    can be known, and defied

Vinegar and honey to
soothe
the throat
as light haloed above us in umber and ochre,
    painter's colors crusted with neglect, we transformed
each dry surface with vessels of water,
steamed rosemary and mint to recharge the
cigarette-fingered perception of   life   indoors, we

Left out bowls of water for
birds and squirrels, bowls
of   water   like   hymns—some
for them
and some for us—and with
    purpose for ten days, we forgot to worry

About the other disaster, fixed
instead on our hollow   of bad air, breath
shallow with careful no-coughs, we kept   still and

kept mouths covered,   certain and manageable, which
reminded us of fire drills: when to   lower
   our bodies, when test doorknobs

The thing is, we won't remember how
it felt, wearing our masks inside,
just like   I didn't remember how
a small boat made its way through my childhood home
      during its second flood,
hovering over brown water

   I wore a mask then, too:
pulled it down to eat a banana the Red Cross
tossed us from their truck after the storm

I didn't even remember that   it had happened until
   I took my mask down to
eat figs thirty years later—some
parts   they keep themselves hidden
certainty is the myth
we let
      go

ENTANGLEMENT

My doctor called them cobwebs
She watched
as a surgeon wrestled loose
the parts of me he was tasked
to remove from the adhesions
none of us expected to be there:
detritus, seaweed tangles, my pelvis
a shipwreck whose rusted bulkheads
gave way to spoils and deep sea gardens

Mass begets mass: O, how my body took from itself, fed
only to regenerate and swallow, that endless creation
of matter, superfluous and thick as lubricant
to flush out an irritant from a cavity
Strangled organs engulfed, wrapped, twisted,
no longer to perform their symphony of systems,
the surgeon twisted each free, my organs scampering
prey foiling a spider's feast. But my doctor made
no promises—not about the pain
nor the future. I like to think of it this way,
for now: a hummingbird tangled up is still a centrifuge
All her life force—ready to unfurl

ART THERAPY

Before discovery, before surgery
        and excavation I planned drawings of
the lava of my middle,
        my pelvic bone rendered in black ink
wide as the Bristol pad which bore it
        I sketched horrors, each pain a retelling
of the hips of my Doomsday
        —all plagues, all infestations:
boxelders for their perseverance;
        larva and flies for their consumption;
grubs for writhing in the rot of me

The truth was these pests heralded
        dormancy, the two-on-a-pain-scale days,
hallelujahs so rare I dared not jinx them
        The truth was, I buried the lede
I was not consumed
        by slow, small beasts of the earth
No, most days were electric eels
        shocking and feasting; tentacles
swift, sharp, and mean; most days
        I was scourged by the stuff
of bad tattoos—razor blades, broken
        glass, barbed wire—none of which
I could bring myself to render

IT GETS YOU THROUGH

Last years' costumes laid to rest in attics and above
armoires, all shimmer of sequins and
plume of feathers hand-glued, our creations
now downy with mildew, stained
in ways we've seen on the walls of every
home we've said grace in.

After the waters rise—*was a flood just one too
many road drinks poured down the front of
something?*—a hum like a beehive, then
silence, the water swells, umber and
grey, it sloshes and ruins and recedes.

Some came to town for carnival and
never left; locals learned how to survive storm
after storm, kept afloat on the promise
of a next year, and next year's
costume, an investment as earnest
as seeds in the ground.

DISASTER PLANNING

I picked Oregon because I was tired of the floods and hurricanes and I didn't pick California because they have their own problems. Dinnertime conversation veers on the edge of disaster preparedness, a quick lick at our heels, each respective phobia laid bare and pedantic. We each fear something larger than ourselves: an almost expected list of plane crash, fire, earthquake, outbreak. I think but don't say, "a driver mowing through the front of our house," an embellished fear born out of a news story of an early-morning drunk driver who took out a hedge of roses and the grandmother who had been weeding her garden beds. Cars always feel like weaponry to me. But instead, I say a house fire, which is also true. We each have our own list of nagging thoughts; we all fret about our stoves combusting when we're anxious about other things. Some demons you can plan for better than others, so we stick to natural-disaster planning—like this game called life is F-U-N. So let's say it's an earthquake. We'll agree to swiftly push the dining room table towards one interior wall. We'll each get a table leg to wrap our entire large bodies around like a koala. If I don't shit myself first, I'd like to grab my motorcycle helmet from the mantle, then the papillon. I'll put on the helmet. There are three other koalas in the room. We each clutch our branch, we each tell something we love, and it goes like this long enough for the shaking to stop.

AUGUST

For Windy

Wild brambles, their bounty hidden
along gravel alleyways clear of shade
we went blackberry picking by bike
& once you showed me
where to look I could never not

Your wrists taught how to approach
the vine without injury, so we tore
& twisted from stems, filled bins
full of plump fruit, inked
fingers darker than wine stains
on our teeth & dusk came so late
that we forgot to eat a real meal

Other nights you'd trespass,
fold your fine limbs & leave
your swift mark on the flanks
of abandoned places that were
to you just as bountiful
as in their prime (how like us, too)
You'd invite me for margaritas
and mischief every summer as if
it'd just occurred to you;

Bless you, for never remembering
my wary decline any better
than whether or not I eat chicken

You're always sneaking
around the rules, my dear
Once you were told you had
less time you even found
a way to de-thorn yourself

Look at our hands, look at our
mouths by the moonlight

Watching you grow old
is already a burst
of fruit in the mouth

THE YEAR I BROKE UP WITH THE MOON

Quick, hook your finger
inside my mouth, rinse the truth
from my teeth, I'll say it was your idea
all hooves, all hips bare, all silvered rooftops

Lycanthropy, cyclical with my possibility
Laparoscopy, 'till our finale
Which is it?
You wore crinoline, permanence
Your folded arms a lesson, you promised
warning before sunrise

Buck Moon, Thunder Moon:
July's full Blood Moon whence I tossed blood
from a tulip, splashed the sidewalk, evoked Jupiter,
evoked Saturn, spat and sifted—it was my birthday
but days were all the same to you—wide bodies
plump with fluid and mine the one with no answers

Beneath window-pane prisms
I stirred stardust, I held
up flanks when it was Time:
to wish; to cast; to remake myself
into that ripe, mortal thing for whom feeding
and fullness was its own reward
You said ritual was good for someone like me

Wolf moon, the sixth, the three-hundred sixtieth,
thirty years incanting: spill, spill, spill
into the sea, cast a net to catch shadows
each swollen part brought by the tide

You mouthed the word Rougarou
and I locked your hair between my palms
Will you call it what it was? (The end of us)

I loathed Pisces for her watery birth
and hot cheeks I spared what I could
after the pills—
no spells, just begging, shrunken parts
foretold what was left of the wolf
I was, radiant heat and that endless waiting, I
checked the faces of clocks and
came as close as I could to prayer:
                                  Believe me when I say that I
                                      tried everything.

I was a flat-backed drought,
knees bent like books, waiting
for the silver dish remedy, tonics
of spice and sky: three crescents
spooned into the night mouth
easy as lycanthropy / laparoscopy

Light came regardless, there was less of me
and the round sameness of you—fed and indifferent

Spit into my mouth for old time's sake
I am all jowls, howling
        Isn't this what you wanted?
You promised
nothing, and reminded me

You knew my impermanence; you whispered
beast, but you never meant it—

FKA PLAQUEMINES

Head of passes, a bird's foot a clenched claw in
clay drudges up the salty remains of
the Mississippi   here my ancestors made homes
& boats of cypress, they knew when to float

    this place is already a work boot
atop an ancient ocean formed & reformed by
the constant recalibration of volume: of
    river, swamp, sea, of
other liquids too   sweet tea & moonshine
calculate the space of absence, that is,   one hundred years
lest the cup of Louisiana drowned   itself
& since: 1,800 square miles of land   gone

       Plaquemines Parish out to sea   the headlines
are poems: one football field   every 100 minutes
   coastal Louisiana 34   square miles of land lost equal to
the expanse of   Manhattan disappearing   annually
wetland   areas   with berms   sediment the   delta
gates & pumps   delayed   perspiration

   latch to what it used to be
land is sponge,   is underwater, is trapped in amber
  with the humidity   primarily marsh,   a moat, an
      underground pillar   gone   colossal

so if humans are 70%   water, are Louisianans putting on
    water weight   to carry the vapor   that used to
be our   state? volume in the   curls & pores   something
  you can   own   your doubt is answered   in the shallow
dig   in the red clay   where water seeps

         we use our hands when measuring
the volume of a
liquid,   our own   capacity, we
          allow the gaps between   fingers &
the wings   of shadow puppets   to hold   tight

SOAK

Our house is clouded over with milk-water,
knee-deep and thick on account of sand and clay
mixed with what we pretend to not know is sewage
In the driveway two children, raisin-fingered, pluck
objects from the deep of a ditch

What I am here to do is siphon water through
a wet vac, shoo the rest out like a toad with my broom
but my instinct is Ophelian: to make a solitary bath
of the master bedroom—no flowers, please—just drywall
as shards of soap, just lower myself down beneath
the window, to clasp the heavy drag of mauve
drapes like reeds, the bottom hem swimming with
me, like mine, suspended in the opaque: just
wet and dry and whatever you call the in between

COMPARTMENTS

My tonsils are soothsayers, their patches of white
are warnings of longer bedrest, worse to come

One doctor tells me:
when things move around, it buys you time
Bodies are elaborate recycling centers, sorting machines

You know what they say
about other people's trash
When they rummaged me
and found delights

A grapefruit appendix
little stones like boba
copper

I get the appeal; I'm part scavenger
searching for gems with skillful fingers
—rot never troubled me

TWO CAPTAINS
A Love Letter to Google Street View

I can tell the temperature of the place by its goldenrod and olive, things taunt
With a light breeze that runs through wispy reeds, water warm and mossy under foot

We begin in Pilottown, La., up and down the South Pass closest to Cuba,
The ochre watercolor runoff from too many brushes, where a bologna eraser smears

The Gulf of Mexico, water glistens but apparatus made flat—this is where
You, you, and the boat are all deleted, as easy as spackle rubbing over the seams

Sky like newsprint, the gulf holds a mirror: shadow-cast by a mechanical buoy
Something hovering above ground, cylindrical and strange: a perch, a box

There's you and you, river crew thick with craft, two captains taking coordinates
With the flick of the wrist, a pocket watch (or is it a compass?) held above the marsh

Obscured, the two yous: one, your light pink cap keeps your face a mystery and
The second you: your fist holds up your face behind gas-station sunglasses

Two captains and four oars in the collage of whoever it is cutting out the details,
Leaving a trail behind of Google Street View where gulf water is a street

The canoe glistens on the surface while you and you survey the marina,
Remnants of docks, cypress wood the way grass seems to grow under water

The rowing, despite appearances of solid, green land is through marsh
Grass and water, an artifice, like calling the skin on the top of gravy a solid

The Gulf is a byproduct, a lifetime of runoff where diluted water stains
The two of you take turns: you with Adonis' curls, and you with a life vest

We're mapping water to understand land. We're watching both vanish, morph,
Change shape. Saltwater and freshwater. There are more than two but that's life.

Which captain would I choose? The beautiful you, or the sensible you?
As if I'd be reduced to digest complexities; clearly, I'd take the both of you.

27

THIS CORROSION BEATS ON

And so do the men we paid to rebuild the
collapsed bones, the stairs that led to our

home, one-hundred years hovering
like a ghost above ground, porch

a perch where someone in a bustle
might've descended from her threshold

seven houses and thirty horse rings down
from the masonic lodge with brazen pillars

we traded twenty-first century American
adult dollars for the use of mens' muscle and wrists

they hammered the frame then poured concrete while
you and I do what we call work but not labor

on computers in bedrooms that we use as offices in the
house we call ours, century-old Douglas firs flattened into

floors, we talk about nothing; we hover between walls, ghosts
ourselves one day, a threat to be buried out back, like pets

Instead I carved our initials into fresh cement with a toothpick,
splashed gold glitter like rice at a wedding to see what would stick,

what the birds might take; wet to permanent,
we poured something and called it ours

I'M BACK AT URGENT CARE IN OVERALLS AGAIN

I'm wearing a lavender gown
and holding up the waist of
my Carhartts with both hands
like I'm in a potato sack race
    —we have to stop meeting like this

The same nurse as last time
greets the scrambled output
of my EKG reading with a too-long silence:
                    Odd
I've never seen it do this before
The gap between
thunder and lightning—I count
the seconds, and she gets the doctor

Who asks gently,
What are you most afraid
this might be, so we
can pay the closest attention
And I answer, my heart.

Have you heard any good news, lately?
Mine came right before this appointment
and this poem; I was eating Taco Bell
in the car during a rainstorm
and a wish of mine was granted

Mostly, it felt good
to want something

MICROCHIMERISM

Go together and go
alone it's the shadow-shape

of you underfoot, by which I mean
it's my shadow that's you-shaped, broad

and hard-lined, an imprint, a rubbing, my
cells from whence they came

the book said fetal cells actively manipulate
the mother from within   and if you knew, you'd

never let me live it down; you'd point them out
like burrs stuck to jeans but you'd let them stay.

    I changed you from the inside then
spent decades adapting to life underneath

extracting my material from you, if only it were the
inheritance of bones without the brain and heart. Peel,

first for survival and tolerance, then for escape, yet I

see you in my reflections and affectations, my
silhouette cast upon places we'll never go alongside

Our shadows and cells shared,
    we've been taking each other everywhere
    whether we wanted to or not.

FIRST THE GRASSHOPPER

You tucked magic into objects, that was one thing
about you. Shenanigans, another. Once, day drunk
on Capitol Hill, we stuffed hot sauce and beer
bottles into the balconies of our bras, a swift smug
grift. Tits hexagonal, we sloshed into the next bar
that was, bless their hearts, willing to serve us.

I keep a short list of things to tell you if you'd haunt
me properly: first the grasshopper, second the jam.

Amanda, I heard men croak out your name in grief,
including the one I love. You slept between us once,
your curls and limekiln body, we rolled glitter into slate sheets.
Did everyone love you this much? That anyone wasn't savoring
their life on account of yours ending gutted you and yet,
after you passed we emerged with hulls scraped bare.

But back to the list. First, the grasshopper I was convinced
was you: persistent and out of season, you were a green thing
I wished for, exiled to our bedroom by lamplight. I curled
a magazine into a cannon, escorted the ancient insect
called by your name outside. *Last call, girl.* Incredible
that you kept finding your way back in.

Second, we still have the clove and berries
you mashed and poured, made panacea with your hands
and encased in glass, metal rim rubbed rust and marked
with black cursive, a date expired. In movies,
when they go to open an ancient vessel the anthropologist
always mouths, *Don't you dare!* Is that their best warning?
Do they know something we don't? If we break
this seal, will some part of you erupt, be ingestible?

First the grasshopper, second the jam, both are you
in the air I just keep thinking about breathing
you in. You, stirring clove into berries
onto cinder cone. An incantation. Throat raw from
combustion, you are the magic thing that is windborne.

WHAT HAPPENS TO THE BOXELDERS AFTER NOVEMBER

11.
The end of light, heralded
by a deluge, by leaves that won't quit
we are half-allure and half-dread, we crawl
into attics for supplies, we prepare for dormancy
then fight against it like the plump squirrel hoarding
what she can. Near the canopy of our Fatsia japonica
Boxelder bugs are harbingers of what is to come, they pulse
alongside verdant fading, rust-tinged with decay
and while we expect the molder of last month's porch pumpkins,
here it is and here is how it begins—what the sun gives
does not match what our bodies need

12.
I am a rain barrel only I am hoarding
light, I use a dumb little lamp that fakes dawn
with birdsong and creamsicle glow
I've left myself notes in the pockets of last winter's robes
and I've reread last winter's poems, still
my garden is already a memory of rot and old roots
where I watch our yard transform
to an austere, skeletal thing—all hard edges

1.
Winter pulls no punches yet I forget
every year how it bleeds, whether the sliver
of fleeting sunbeams must strike my skin
to count—I am so soup-thick that I don't know
how to phrase it: If my indoor plants are fooled
by lightbulbs and continue to sprout new leaves,
can I too be a simple, green thing? Winter, when

I have also forgotten brassy summer days
at the bluffs, strewn bicycles, bodies so cherry-fresh
and mine freckled, basking in that persistent glow
atop a blanket where we watch sunset after sunset
drop ice cubes and berries into mason jars
full of rosé, summer when I don't think
once about the arrival of Boxelder bugs,
how the little ones shine, bright red as holly

DEPARTURES

When she said she wanted a head start, she meant *I pulled
my stitches out with my teeth.* That's one way to move out
of state: load up the truck, call the kids from a payphone

Your way, another—without a word. Grief in the rear-view
though you forgot to check the backseat, called home
like a migratory bird—the drawl of your aaaah's
a cacophonous Lawd!—you shed the last crust
of boyhood then changed your zip code

I think I'd like to do some leaving, too
except I am locksmith and proprietrix, my metal
to stay put. Bolted seams of worn lock
and warped key, this mess of loving
shadows in lieu of farewells

—the lesson I am teaching
myself before the next time:
when to lock up, when to hand
over the tangle, and when
to swallow the keys

ACKNOWLEDGMENTS

We are on this land because of the forced removal of its traditional peoples by colonists and settlers. I take this opportunity to also acknowledge the indigenous caretakers of this land, as an acknowledgment to the land and/or territories these poems were written on or inspired by, as a way to recognize and pay my respect and gratitude for their stewardship of these lands—past, present and future. In particular:

Oregon: The unceded lands of the Confederated Tribes of Grand Ronde and the Confederated Tribes of Siletz Indians, specifically on the lands of the Clackamas and Cowlitz peoples. What we now call Portland, Oregon and Multnomah County are the ancestral lands of the Multnomah, Wasco, Kathlamet, Clackamas, Cowlitz, bands of Chinook, Tualatin Kalapuya, Molalla and many other Tribes who made their homes along the Columbia and Willamette Rivers.
Florida: The unceded lands held by the Ais, Apalachee, Calusa, Timucua, Tocobago, Seminole, Miccosukee Tribes/Nations.
Louisiana: The traditional village sites of communities of Caddo Adai Indians of Louisiana, Biloxi Chitimacha Confederation, Louisiana Choctaw Tribe/Choctaw Nation, Jena Band of Choctaw Indians, Choctaw-Apache Community of Ebarb, Coushatta, Four Winds Tribe-Louisiana Cherokee Confederacy, Muscogee (Creek), Pointe-Au-Chien Tribe, United Houma Nation, Grand Bayou Indian Village and the Atakapa-Ishak/Chawasha Tribe of Plaquemines Parish, Acolapissa, Grand Caillou/Dulac Band, Isle de Jean Charles Band, Tunica Biloxi Tribe, and others.

Gratitude to the following journals, in which these poems first appeared (at times in slightly modified versions):

Bayou Magazine: "Two Captains" | *Cheat River Review:* "The Names of Streets" | *DMQ:* "Cut off, La" | *Gaze:* "The swamp is a third-gender thing" | *Gigantic Sequins:* "First The Grasshopper" | Honey Literary: "Mt Tabor" | *Juke Joint:* "Mildew" | *Muzzle:* "Smoke Water" | *No Contact:* "Disaster Planning" | *Poetry Shore:* "This Corrosion Beats On" | *Rejection Letters:* "Untitled Garden Poem" | *Rougarou:* "Soak" | *Soundings East:* "It Gets You Through" | *Southern Humanities:* "FKA Plaquemines" | *Sweet Lit:* "Departures" (formerly "Head Start") | *Vagabond City:* "I'm Back At Urgent Care In Overalls Again" | *Welter:* "Art Therapy"

Rhienna Renée Guedry (she/they) is a writer, illustrator, and producer whose favorite geographic locations all have something to do with their proximity to water. A two-time Pushcart Prize nominee and 2022 Tin House Workshop alum, her work has appeared in *Muzzle*, *Maudlin House*, *Gigantic Sequins*, *HAD*, and elsewhere. Rhienna is currently working on her first novel. Find out more about her projects at rhienna.com.

www.ingramcontent.com/pod-product-compliance
Lightning Source LLC
Chambersburg PA
CBHW030141100526
44592CB00011B/990